# 7-Day Money Empowerment D.I.E.T.

DISCIPLINE

INNOVATION

EMPOWERMENT

TRANSFORMATION

**ERIC AND TAMAR GOODSON**

Copyright 2021 by Eric and Tamar Goodson

All rights reserved.

No part of this book may be reproduced in any form or by any electronic or mechanical means including information storage and retrieval systems, except in the case of brief quotations embodied in critical articles or reviews-without permission in writing from its publisher (The Legacy Empowerment Group).

Disclaimer: The information contained in this book is based on the authors' experience, knowledge, and opinions. The author and publisher will not be held liable for the use or misuse of the information in this book.

ISBN# 978-1-7373240-9-6

https://legacyppa.com

For speaking engagements or signed or bulk orders, email: admin@legacyppa.com

Cover and interior design: Deborah Perdue: https:illuminationgraphics.com

Editor: Margaret A. Harrell: https://margaretharrell.com

Published by

# Dedication

To the many money coaching clients, both individuals and couples, across the country and the world, who have sat face to face and knee to knee with us during our sessions and workshops since 2016. Your passion, enthusiasm and taking the message of Money Coaching to new heights, changing behaviors, breaking generational trends, and restoring families and hope across the world.

To Deborah Price, Founder of The Money Coaching Institute, our mentor, leader, and mama bear. Your dedication and vision to empower us over the years has not only change our lives but the lives of those whom we had the honor to work with. Your vision for what CMC's could become turned our small local company into a worldwide household name. Millions of families thank you –
and so do we.

# Acknowledgements

Writing a book is a huge endeavor that goes far beyond the names on the cover. We'd like to thank the following people for empowering the change to make this book possible.

Margaret Harrell, our editor for this book, for helping us turn years' worth of teaching, experience, and empowerment into a manual that anyone can use to win with money.

Deborah Perdue, for overseeing all design, cover art, and project management support. And for letting us know what worked – and what didn't.

# Preface

How to Transform Yourself—*From the Inside out*

The 7-day Money Empowerment is a guide to support you on all levels where money is concerned.

If you are stuck and cannot understand your thoughts about money and/or your behavior or pattern, read on!

# Introduction

This book is a 7-day money-empowerment guide to support you in renewing your mind around money. Whether you are aware or unaware of your money patterns and/ or behaviors, you will be given the jump start and motivation needed to take inventory of your money thoughts. You will gain awareness for the next 7 days how to be conscious on all levels about money. It is nearly impossible to master your money world without becoming conscious on all levels of your existence and experience with Money.

When we first learned about our money archetypes from owner/founder Deborah Price from the Money Coaching Institute where we became Certified Money Coaches, we were blown away and scared at the same time. As we finally started understanding our money triggers, we had a lot of work to do. We literally made the worst mistakes with money anyone could on the face of the planet. We were in a vicious cycle and did not know how to get out. We learned budgeting, which did not work. We tried so many ways to get out of debt. The harder we tried, the worst things got. Foreclosure, bankruptcy, repossessions—you name it, we have experienced it all. We were slowly drowning, unable to help each other. We literally had to learn to relax in the middle of the ocean and allow the waves of life to carry us.

We wrote this book to share with you some small but very significant steps that will provide some practical ways to think about money. You cannot keep pouring old wine into a new wineskin. You must replenish the wineskin before new wine can be poured in.

If you do not know how you think about money or how money manages you, how can you ever fix your money problems?

That is precisely what was wrong with us until we got to the root of the problem—it was our hard wire around money. No wonder we made money but were unable to ever manage it. We were like baskets without bottoms. This book will help you take inventory, dig a little into your history, and survey your current situation where money is concerned.

This is an important step to take. Most marriages and other relationships must face this money topic. How you respond will make a world of difference. Often, we are reacting because we simply don't understand ourselves. What triggered us goes unnoticed, and boom here comes the blame, shame, guilt, projection. Even though the problem is there, we can't seem to grip the notion that perhaps we just need help—another form of help. But very frequently paralysis steps in, as we honestly don't know what questions to ask.

Be prepared to be empowered beyond measure. We are here to go a little deeper with you. Leave all your self-judgement at the door and let's get to the bottom of this money thing once and for all.

DAY 1

# Where Did I Learn About Money?

Date: _____

## My Mental Presence

What do I think about money? How was my mind impacted from childhood about money? When was the first time I encountered, learned, became aware of, touched money? What was my experience with money?

_____

_____

_____

_____

_____

_____

_____

_____

_____

_____

_____

## My Emotional Presence

How do I feel about money? How do I identify with money? Does having plenty of money make me feel happy? Or can I be happy with very little money? How much of my happiness depends on money?

## My Physical Presence

What do I spend my money on? Do I associate what I own, what I drive, or where I live with money? Do I dress according to how much money I have or don't have?

## My Spiritual Presence

How do I spend my money?
Do I believe I should tithe or give donations
to church and to charity?
What kinds of things do I buy?

_____

_____

_____

_____

_____

_____

_____

_____

_____

_____

_____

**Empowerment Supplement:**

Money is energy.

So it is important to identify the energy you carry in your mind and behavior around money.

**Consciousness:**

When you start to think about money on these levels—Mental, Emotional, Physical, and Spiritual—you will begin to understand money and the impact it has on you daily from a conscious place. You will begin to locate and understand your behavior around money much more. You may find that you have a need to go shopping if you are sad. If you are angry, you might just disregard your budget that you have worked so hard on and begin to fall into an archetype that does not serve your higher good (see https://legacyppa.com and take your money quiz to learn more about your active archetypes). Being aware of what makes you spend the way you spend or save the way you save will be gratifying. Where your money is concerned, you will finally be in control.

# DAY 2

# What Do I Remember?

Date: _____

## My Mental Presence

Who do you think you behave more like now with money (Father, Mother, Grandparents, Guardian, etc.)?

_____

_____

_____

_____

_____

_____

_____

_____

_____

_____

_____

_____

_____

DAY 2

## My Emotional Presence

How do you feel about money now? Does money make you angry, sad, mad, happy, depressed, paralyzed in your mind, a deer in the headlight?

_____

_____

_____

_____

_____

_____

_____

_____

_____

_____

_____

## My Physical Presence

What was it like, growing up? Did you have access to physical money? How was money disclosed or spoken of as you were growing up?

_____

_____

_____

_____

_____

_____

_____

_____

_____

_____

_____

## My Spiritual Presence

Was God/Spirituality a major part of my parent's life and how did they manage money?

_____

_____

_____

_____

_____

_____

_____

_____

_____

_____

_____

_____

**Empowerment Supplement:**

We can choose to keep
some early background and
dispose of other things
that do not serve us now.

## Power Talk:

Our parents are our mirrors. As children, we learn everything from the adults in our lives: nonverbal, intentional, taught, or not taught. A lot of people would say, "My parents didn't teach me anything about money." However, that statement might not be as accurate as you think. Take inventory now of what you remember about the adults in your life growing up, see if you can find some similarities.

Here is the deal—watch the animals. They learn from their parents or others in their species. So do we. Everyone had to learn from someone. Taking the time to remember how your parents were with money is vital to finding the root cause of your engrained/hardwire relationship with money—the underlying assumptions. Look around you now and examine what might be a habit you weren't aware of that you may have inherited.

# DAY 3

# Who Am I Without Money?

Date: _____

## My Mental Presence

What is my most dominant thought about money?

_____

_____

_____

_____

_____

_____

_____

_____

_____

_____

_____

## My Emotional Presence

How has money caused me to feel when I have it and when I do not?

## My Physical Presence

Where will my money take me?

## My Spiritual Presence

Is money my God?

**Empowerment Supplement:**

Do you find yourself freaking out when your bank account gets low? For a few months whenever the opportunity presents itself, observe yourself. That will tell you who you are with money or without it.

You are more than money. You are more valuable than money. Do not allow anyone to treat you poorly because you have less than. Do not treat others without respect because you have more money than they do.

## Power Talk:

Have you been treated badly because it was clear that someone had more money than you? Have you treated anyone badly because you had more money than they did? Either way, if any of those two scenarios was true of you, it is simply an indication that you have a bad relationship with money. You are a puppet, and money is your master at this point, or you are enslaved. If this statement is a bother to you, well, there goes the red flag and clear indicator that—it's time to get to the root of the problem and change your master. If you treat others poorly because you have money, it's still your master, and if you allow others to treat you poorly because you do not have a lot of money, then you are enslaved and/or governed by it. If you are governed by money and see nothing wrong with that, try imagining being among the large number of Have Nots. See if maybe you can find a notion in your mind that—that behavior is caused by insecurities and a host of other things. Either way, folks, Self-Empowerment, through money coaching, is a wonderful, effective, results-producing way to start.

# DAY 4

# Ownership

Date: _____

## My Mental Presence

How do I handle money? Am I comfortable talking about money with friends and family? Do I know how to budget? balance my checkbook?

_____

_____

_____

_____

_____

_____

_____

_____

_____

_____

_____

_____

## My Emotional Presence

Today, I acknowledge I may not have the best habits when it comes to finances. How does this make you feel?

_____

_____

_____

_____

_____

_____

_____

_____

_____

_____

_____

_____

## My Physical Presence

Have I taken an inventory of the things I spend my money on? This tells me a lot about how I relate to money. About who is important to me and what is important to me. Who is? What is?

_____

_____

_____

_____

_____

_____

_____

_____

_____

_____

_____

_____

_____

## My Spiritual Presence

I forgive myself for all the things I need to change about my money habits and would like to change. Make a list of the things that you forgive yourself for, as well as a list of the things that you would like to change.

**Empowerment Supplement:**

You are the master of your own life. God honors the words that comes out of your mouth. Your actions are important after your change of heart.

**Power Talk:**

"Ownership" is a big word, right? This is where being responsible comes in, the call for a plan of action, implementation, and execution. This is where the work begins. Ownership of my own relationship with money come into play. Ownership annihilates all excuses, blame, and/or guilt we carry every day. Ownership says, "I can. Yes, I can, and I will." Ownership acknowledges the roadblocks, the bad experiences, but ownership rises above them all. Ownership gives hope and motivates simultaneously.

# DAY 5

# Forgive

Date: _____

## My Mental Presence

I see that money plays a big part in my decisions. Being aware now, how will I choose to be more mindful of how I make my choices, as I now can tap into my mental presence where money is concerned?

## My Emotional Presence

It feels great to know—in fact, be sure—I can change my relationship with money. What do I plan to implement in my life that can change my relationship with money?

_____

_____

_____

_____

_____

_____

_____

_____

_____

_____

_____

## My Physical Presence

My physical position does not own me, or dictate who I am, or where I want to go, and who I even aspire to be. Remove all the limits in your life and ask yourself, what do I truly want?

_____

_____

_____

_____

_____

_____

_____

_____

_____

_____

_____

_____

_____

## My Spiritual Presence

Help me, God, to see myself as more valuable than money. Make a list of all the people, life achievements, and things in your life that's more valuable to you than money.

_____

_____

_____

_____

_____

_____

_____

_____

_____

_____

_____

As you appreciate your life today, know that God your creator loves you so much. Feel that now. Imagine that now. Breathe that in this moment.

**Empowerment Supplement:**

Take control of your life and dictate on each level what you will be.

## Power Talk:

Whether you grew up wealthy or poor, money is NOT more important than you—yes, you are PRICELESS! Many of us, poor or wealthy, have been manipulated by money. Our parents perhaps, if we are wealthy, paid us off with things, versus spending quality time with us. If we were poor, our parents perhaps were too busy working and being overwhelmed with being poor to show how much they prized us. Maybe even to instill that love factor. As you will come to understand, money is a means of exchange. It was created by our human society to trade in a more structured, organized way. Before money, there was the bartering system. When you exchanged one item for another item (with no money exchanged), it was easier to value each other because you had more opportunity to learn each other's specific gift as you traded your item or work for the other person's item or work. Nevertheless, we are here now, where money is our currency. Remember to see yourself independent of money, and then you can truly see how precious you are.

# DAY 6

# **Accountability**

Date: _____

## My Mental Presence

Today I choose to write out all my thoughts around money.

_____

_____

_____

_____

_____

_____

_____

_____

_____

_____

_____

_____

## My Emotional Presence

No matter what my feelings are today about money and with money, I know that the power is within me to change. How can I manage my money in a way that truly demonstrate my essence?"

## My Physical Presence

Today is cleaning day.
What have I been spending my money on that does not serve me?

_____

_____

_____

_____

_____

_____

_____

_____

_____

_____

_____

## My Spiritual Presence

My spirit has no ties with money, so I release the pain money has caused me. Make a list of circumstances, events, relationships, transaction, or traumas that money may have caused you pain, and then release them ALL!

_____

_____

_____

_____

_____

_____

_____

_____

_____

_____

_____

_____

**Empowerment Supplement:**

Until you realize that you are a spirit made up of three parts, you will treat yourself as only flesh and blood. You have a spirit that wears an earth suit, your physical self. You have a mind that thinks thoughts (mental body or mental self). You have a soul that governs your emotions.

Your spirit was created for a purpose.

**Power Talk:**

Do you now know that you need accountability in one or more areas of your life? Money is still a very touchy subject. Only with accountability will we be able to learn new habits around money. Because we have been programed for most of our lives unconsciously around money, we will need an extra accountability plan or person to help us to consciously choose our new way of relating to money. You do not necessarily have to start out with a bad relationship with money to benefit from learning your money identity. To learn your psychological money patterns will empower you, regardless.

# DAY 7

# Empowerment

Date: _____

## My Mental Presence

Today is a new day for me. I am free to learn how to manage my money. I have done my unlearning and acknowledged where I was. What do I plan to do daily to create positive empowering thought with relationship with money?

_____

_____

_____

_____

_____

_____

_____

_____

_____

_____

_____

## My Emotional Presence

Today, I can no longer allow my emotions to lead me where money is concerned. Money is a real thing, and I have based my use of it on how I felt, which was a sabotage and real trick of the Fool Money Archetype—(to learn more about the money archetypes please visit: https://legacyppa.com and take the free Money type Quiz) Use this acronym for MONEY (My Own Natural Energy Yields) to assist you with completing the following. What are some ways that you've been sabotaging yourself where money is concerned? What are you going to do differently?

_____

_____

_____

_____

_____

*(Continue Journaling next page)*

## My Emotional Presence

(Continued)

## My Physical Presence

Today, choose to stand in this empowerment of doing your work over the past few days. If you could do your "money life" over again, what would you do differently?

_____

_____

_____

_____

_____

_____

_____

_____

_____

_____

_____

_____

## My Spiritual Presence

Today, be fully aware that you were guided to this book by your spirit. Be thankful and continue to grow and be the best version of yourself. What is your next step? How do you plan to improve your financial situation?

_____

_____

_____

_____

_____

_____

_____

_____

_____

_____

_____

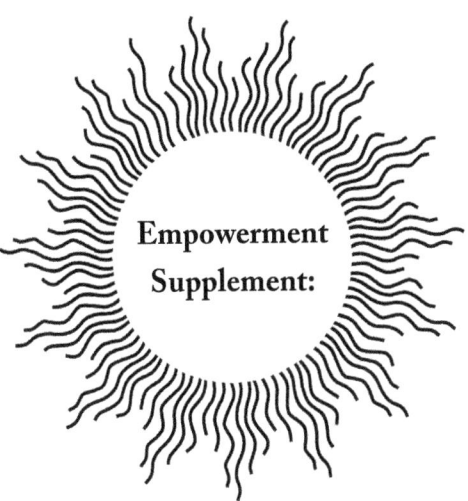

**Empowerment Supplement:**

It's never too late to start.

## Power Talk:

True empowerment begins from inside. The *root* is where the cause is located. You go there to find the cause. Upon finding it, you can remedy the situation by your response. Your response will be from a place of true empowerment if you can start from the inside out. Patterns develop from practice. Unlearning, in order to learn a new way, means you must go deeper.

## THE PRACTICE OF ACTIVE INTENTION
*(Recite as often as needed)*

## MY PRAYER OF INTENTION

To feel and know God's presence. To know that there is no separation between God and myself.
To surrender all fear, doubt and worry, and to simply trust God.
To surrender all judgment about myself and others, and to live in a state of compassion, acceptance and love.
To forgive EVERYTHING AND EVERYONE, INCLUDING MYSELF.
To have clarity of purpose.
To have clarity of heart.
To have clarity of mind.
To be a conscious co-creator with God.
To live in complete collaboration and celebration of the divinity that exists within myself and each of us.
To be joyful and live in a state of grace and bliss.
To know all my needs are always met.
To soften in any place that I have become hardened.
To live the truth, speak the truth, and see the truth.
To be of service to God and humanity.
To GIVE MY GIFT.

*Continued on next page...*

To LET GO OF FEAR.
To be healthy and strong.
To allow myself to be taken care of.
To be a generous giver and a gracious receiver.
To be the best father, mother, grandparent, son, daughter, neighbor, co-worker that I can possibly be.
To be the best friend and partner/spouse that I can possibly be.
To graciously receive my divine inheritance and experience prosperity and abundance throughout my life.
To BEING the best version of myself that I can possibly be.

Be Blessed and Empowered Beyond Measure!

# Conclusion

Over the past years, we've led many individuals and families through our Money Coaching sessions and classes, which unpacks all the baby Steps, information, and practical application that we've covered throughout this book. We're not bragging here. We really say that just to let you know that the stuff we teach isn't new, and it isn't some crackpot theory about how we think money works. It's a time-proven system that's been tested and changed the lives of thousands of individuals and families around the world.

This stuff works, and we didn't invent any of it. We just took the time. Intention to learn, did our work, and packaged it well for others to start their journey. We truly believe that the material we teach is God's way of handling ourselves with money. God worked these lessons out in our own lives through fire and adversity. The truth is, we couldn't have earned them any other way. Once all our assumptions about wealth were totally stripped away as we went broke, once we literally had nothing left but our family and a willing spirit, God picked us up and led us down this path of self-discovery. On that journey, we learned things about God, money, relationships, and our life's calling. It's amazing what God can do with a wiling spirit. This stuff changed our lives, and we pray that it changes yours too. We can walk with you and hold your hands through the process, but it's up to you to take the first step.

# Afterword

This book gives you a good start on multiple levels to make a shift towards transforming from the inside out where money is concerned. But no book alone can do much to completely change thought and behavior patterns. We believe that the properly led small group is hands down the best method we've ever experience for doing that. There's just something powerful about sitting face to face with other's and working through this together. When you go through this material with other men and women, the shame and mystery behind the money curtain starts to melt away. You truly get to witness that you're not alone, no matter where you are in your journey. Everybody makes mistakes. Everybody has done stupid things with money. Everybody is capable of being empowered beyond measure. Sometimes that's hard to see if you're just sitting home alone, reading a book.

f you have not attended one of our Money Coaching sessions or workshops, you should. With the support of technology, we are able to have sessions and classes throughout the United States and across the world. It is truly six weeks that can change your life. And if you have gone through the class, we encourage you to do it again! We could even start a mastermind group/class in your area and help other families experience the money empowerment you've discovered! It's a great way to spend one night a week.

For more information contact us at
admin@legacyppa.com
we look forward to hearing from you.

# Contact us:

www.LegacyPPA.com

Email: admin@legacy.com
Follow us on Facebook @

www.ingramcontent.com/pod-product-compliance
Lightning Source LLC
Chambersburg PA
CBHW071814160426
43209CB00003B/78